It's Okay to Love Again

Emilie Lancour

Copyright © 2023 Emilie Lancour

No portion of this book may be reproduced in any form without written permission from the publisher or author, except as permitted by U.S. copyright law.

All contents of this book are based on my experiences, memories, and journal writing. Some names are changed to protect privacy.

Cover art by Emilie Lancour @upuneditedphotography

Author picture by Lisa Marie Anderson Photography

Published by Emilie Lancour, Hancock, MI

ISBN: 978-1-7346723-4-3(Paperback)

First Edition 2023

Printed in the United States of America

All rights reserved.

I dedicate this book to Steve, my first love of a lifetime and to Chris, the man I plan to grow old and gray with. I will love both of you, even when we're ghosts.

Background Information

I got married to Steve in 1997 after dating from our junior year in high school through college. We were raising three boys, Michael, Brian, and Matthew together. Michael had started dating a girl named Skylar. We had added on to our house a couple of years before with plans to live here until we were both old and maybe would need in-home health care. We talked about the future. We planned to take a honeymoon for our 25th anniversary. We talked about what we would do in a few years when we were both eligible to retire from teaching. We had talked about what would happen if he passed away after unexpectedly losing a friend.

In December 2018, Steve needed to have routine surgery. He was a teacher and so scheduled it for a Monday before Christmas break to not have to take more than a couple of days of school off and he would heal before the holiday and be able to return in January. We talked about how worried he was. I told him it was very routine and that I was sending a prayer for it to go well. The surgery went well.

On Tuesday, I returned to work and the kids returned to school. We left that morning thinking everything was fine. We were called to the hospital that afternoon to find out that he had passed away. After an in-depth investigation, the autopsy report showed fatty liver disease and was not connected to the surgery. I think it was his time and God had a plan.

I was in total shock, grief, and disbelief. I had no idea how to be a single mom of three. I wasn't confident in myself. I had no idea how not to be Steve's partner. We had spent a huge majority of our lives together. I didn't know how to make decisions by myself. I didn't know what was best for me or the boys.

Since then, I have learned to trust myself and to do what is best for me and my children. I wrote a lot in a journal each day. I asked questions. I spent time asking God how this could be his plan and what my future would hold. I worked through the grief and found a new normal through my faith, my writing, counseling, and a lot of support from family and friends.

In 2020 I wrote a memoir, called "It's Okay to be Okay, Finding Joy Through Grief" as a way to heal and let others know that although you will also grieve and miss the person you lost, you can also be happy and experience joy and peace.

2020 brought a lot of changes to who I am as a person and in my confidence level. I started to really think about the future and if I was okay with being alone. I made it through two years. The second year was worse than the first. I think I was still in shock in the first year. Then reality hits and the truth that he will not be coming back sets in. My boys were growing into young men.

I had a new job. I had new friends. I had new self-care routines. Maybe I was becoming ready for some other changes in the form of a relationship.

I am writing this book from texts, messages, conversations, and journal writings, to let others know that it is okay to move forward. You can find love after the loss of the love of your lifetime. You can find someone to be with until your lungs give out.

Prologue

In the past couple of months, I have realized that I've accepted Steve's death and I'm okay. I'm even good most days. I completely accept that everyone is in their time frame and there are no rules to this grief journey, but I also know that I cannot stay in a place of grief. I must move forward, not only for my boys, who have kept me going but for myself. I have the right to be happy. I have the right to be sad, to miss Steve, and to grieve the loss of the marriage we had and the memories we won't create. I have the right to do activities by myself or go out to dinner with a friend.

My newest right I'm realizing is the right to look for someone else to fall in love with. I have done a lot of praying and a lot of journaling to decide to move forward. Who I am now is because of who I have been in my past and the events that have happened. I believe that God has put me here to love others, to be accepting, and to experience absolute joy. He has given me the strength to suffer through and survive loss, grief, and heartbreak.

When my friend Tacy died in 2010, Steve and I talked about people moving forward and getting remarried and what the time frame should be. She was the same age we were and it was shocking to think about our marriage ending because of sudden death. We agreed that we had no idea how long it would be or if we would ever try to be with someone else if it was us in that situation. There is no time frame other than what is right for each person.

At that time I wrote a note to Tacy's husband telling him, "I thought about how I feel and if it's okay that it is happening already. As I said before, I don't have a definition for "rush into it". I have no idea what it means or how long is "long enough". Here is my conclusion: I never dated anyone other than Steve and he never dated anyone other than me. I have no past loves to remember and never had to move on and start over. I assume that you loved someone before and that it was weird to be with her and not be with the other person at first and then the past became the past and you lived in the present and planned for the future. I never had to do that and so I have no idea how to do it….and I can't imagine trying. I think you moving on means you are coping and living in the present. I am not getting to the present as fast as others and I think that is okay too. I will catch up eventually and if not we will all be at different places. The song I wrote for Brian (my son) when he was born has the line, "In our hearts, a new space grew". I think that is what is happening now. No one can replace her. Her space is taken. But a new space grows and gets filled with someone else and new memories are formed. I believe that you can love more than one person. I have three boys and although I love them all and

I love them the same amount, the love is different with each one. I love my family and I love Steve. I love my friends. All of these loves are different."

Since Steve died, numerous people have sent me a YouTube video about moving forward not moving on. The speaker, Nora McInerny, in the Ted Talk video talks about losing her first husband, Aaron, and the life she has with her current husband, Matthew. I agree with Nora so much when she says that her late husband is present in her marriage to Matthew, because Aaron's life and love, and death made her the person that Matthew wanted to be with. "So I've not moved on from Aaron, I've moved forward with him."

She closes her Ted talk by saying, to remind people that some things can't be fixed and not all wounds are meant to heal. My favorite quote of hers is "that you can and will be sad, and happy; you'll be grieving, and able to love in the same year or week, in the same breath...if they're lucky, they'll even find love again. But yes, absolutely, they're going to move forward. But that doesn't mean that they've moved on."

So much of what she says is exactly where I am feeling. I am ready to live. I'm ready to experience joy. I am ready to experience love. I am ready to experience heartbreak if that's what happens. I am not ready to move on but I am ready to move forward.

I am moving forward, but I am not forgetting.

One Month Gone

January 25, 2018

I hate to be alone. How am I going to do this once all of the kids leave? Can I be okay in this house? Because we planned, we had enough to pay it off so that if I or the kids needed it we could stay or if emotions made it hard, we could move. Right now I need to live here. I need the memories, the projects, our room, and his stuff and although I may take over his closet, I'm not ready to let go yet.

Steve knows that I loved him and that I was and am his love of a lifetime. I still assume mine too. I can't see myself getting married again. Who? How? why? To not be alone is not a good reason. To be happy? I'm not sure it would make me happy. I feel like I was cheating or having an affair and not committed solely to a new person because of my love for Steve.

50 Years?

January 28th, 2018

It's so weird how neither of us ever changed since we were engaged. He still tried to fix everything and I still cry and write more than I talk. I guess since we got together and we were that way, that's why it worked for us. I can't believe he's gone. Way too soon. What happened to us making it to 50 or 70 years of marriage? I'm not sure I can count more years even though I feel we are still married and I don't want to be with anybody else.

Still Feel Married

February 18th, 2018

I still really feel married and it's hard to check the box on forms that say single when I don't feel that way. I feel like if I was to date or kiss or anything, it would be an affair and very wrong.

Jealousy

February 9th, 2019

I just read an issue about joy and being grateful for ourselves and for others even when they get what we wish we had. So when I see a couple kiss I can feel joy for them because they have that relationship and I can feel the joy that I had the chance to experience that with Steve. I still feel jealous of people kissing or holding hands. I still really miss the physical part of my marriage. Especially him hugging me.

Lonely

July 12th, 2019

I went to bed feeling lonely. I cuddled with my quill throughout the night. I woke up still feeling lonely.

Not Ready for Romance

October 15th, 2019

Last night I pulled an angel oracle card and it had the angel of romance on it. It says that I'm going to have romance in my life and to be open to it. I don't think I'm opposed to romance in my life but not now. It's not even been a year. I would like to have somebody to be with in old age, but don't feel ready to be romantic with somebody. It feels like cheating or having an affair. It would be so weird to be with somebody else when I was only ever with Steve; my first everything.

What Do You Want

January 21st, 2020

Yesterday my friend asked me what I wanted for myself.

If I could have anything I wanted it would be love, comfort, companionship, cuddling, dinner, and a movie. Maybe a date night together. To feel loved and attractive and wanted. Somebody who also doesn't know what should or could happen. I know Steve's not coming back. I know he wants me to be happy. I know he'd be okay with being with someone else but how? How do I start? How do I know? How does it work? What if it's awful? What if it makes me feel worse? What if they can't see past my scars, my fat, my tattoo in honor of Steve and just see me? What if I cry through it all? Where do I meet someone who will get my story?

Dear Lord,

Help me have confidence in myself and my looks and self-image and my ability to be a friend and a lover. Help me be with somebody who can love me knowing my story; who can help me learn new things. Help me put all my trust in you that what will happen is meant to be. Help my future date be prayerful too and also trusting and a little self-doubtful. Help me know when the time is right to start something with someone else. Help me know if a relationship can be okay. Help me feel safe physically and emotionally. Help me be honest and loving, careful and strong.

Amen

Switch

January 16th, 2020

A huge switch is happening in my brain. I'm thinking about wanting to be in a relationship. I hope it's not just because I'm lonely. I don't want to be in a relationship or get married because I am feeling alone.

What I Want for Myself

May 23rd, 2019

I want to spend more time at the beach. I want to dance and have fun. I want to learn to believe in myself. I want to find someone to love me so I'm not alone. I want to go to Scotland. I want to be an amazing mom. I want to be liked. I want to be a published author. I want to share my faith and grief.

Living in Love Challenge

June 30th, 2020

I'm doing a 5-day living in love challenge and day one was to listen and describe three things you want and create a vision statement.

To love myself as I gain confidence, except my past as the past and be ready to move forward with new love.

Day two was to break it apart and put those things into action. To love myself as I gain confidence: I need to love who I am, my story, my growth, my love for Steve, our love for each other and my body as it is. My brain tends to overthink everything in my heart that wants to love everyone. To be able to know what I want and not worry about what others think or going to say or feel about her. My past as my past: my relationship with Steve is over. I will never again get to say or here I love you. I will never again feel his touch. I will never wake up with him. I will never forget the love we shared and it has formed me into who I am today and who will be in another relationship. I can't change any of it. I can't go back and do it differently. I can't be different. I can feel different about it. It was all for the purpose of making me who I am, how I see love, and how I view relationships. Be ready to move forward with new love: I don't need permission from anyone to love a new person. I will be loved if this is the choice I make.

My family has always welcomed new loves. You could never have too many people to love you.

I am lonely. I am alone. I miss having somebody to go out to eat with and to watch movies with, to laugh with, and to be intimate with. I don't even know who the new person will be but they will accept the fact that I've only ever been with Steve, that I've had three babies and I have a tattoo. That I'm nervous to be physical with somebody but also that I'd like to try. Many people say that it's different but fun to be with somebody else. Steve, are you good with me wanting to try a new thing? To be with somebody else?

Steve, I know that you're not coming back and that you know me better than anyone else and that I'll pick somebody who will treat me right - like you did. I don't know about getting married again and I don't know how to feel about intimacy. I know you'll continue to watch over me. I want to feel the love we had again. I want somebody to want me and to want to be friends. I want that feeling.

Know Me and My Story

March 14th, 2020

After a conversation with my counselor, I'm wondering why I feel I need to be with somebody who knows my story. Maybe because Steve knew my story before we started dating so maybe because that's all I've ever known that's what I think it should be. She said that she knows a lot of people who have relationships through online dating websites. I don't know if I'm ready for that, which means maybe I'm not ready to date at all. I do wonder how much of this is just the physical piece. Not being hugged or cuddled is really hard. I have tried to do things to take care of my body such as myofascial release, the chiropractor, and massage but it's just not the same as the physical relationship you have with your spouse.

Control of the Future

May 5th, 2020

We don't have control of the future. We can only control how you act to what is happening right now. The past is done. We can't regret it. It has formed us into who we are today and helps us guide the choices we make now. God is always in control. God knows what we need. Maybe the situations are preparing me for something else and these messages will help me accept myself and be able to be in a relationship that's meant to be.

Facebook Group

May 24th, 2020

One of the Facebook groups I'm in is for widows. I wonder how much of it is for when you are a couple of years out from the grief of your spouse. It seems like many are healing or healed. Some people are dating. I wonder about dating.

A friend and I have been talking about maybe starting a relationship, but he has decided that he needs too much counseling and time that he doesn't want me to have to wait. I'm not sure I want to try to be with anyone else. I'm not even sure I want to try dating. I'm not even sure how to do it.

I had a good conversation with a friend today. She told me that because I loved Steve in the relationship we had, that I am probably ready to be in a new relationship. Because the love I have will help me. And it will be different than being with Steve, but it's also okay. She told me that I was a good person and that she's proud of how confident and honest I am. I did feel confident saying what I needed to say.

Learning and Accepting

June 19th, 2020

I'm learning and accepting that it's okay to know what I want and to have an opinion but at the same time see that others have opinions and that we're almost always right. We do the best we can with what we know and when we know it. We move to do better. Steve, I will always love you. You will always have my love but I wonder if it's time to try to be in a relationship with someone else. Different, yet okay. I know I won't be able to have what we did and because it's making me cry means maybe I'm not really ready. I miss so much of you. Of us.

What I Want

July 2nd, 2020

Here is what I know and want:
   A man can love me.
   A man can want me.
   A man will understand and accept my past.
   A man would love me.
   A man will want to be with me.
   A man will teach me to love.
   A man will listen.
   A man will ask about my feelings.
   A man will respect that I own my grief.
   A man will take me to dinner and watch movies.
   A man will check in on me.
   A man will kiss my neck.
   A man will meet up with me.
   A man will accept my independence.
The man and I will each have our own time, friends and activities.

Moving On

July 4, 2020

I don't know about moving on and I don't know how to know if I'm ready either. I guess it's just another thing that there's not a rule book for.

Ready to Date?

July 9th, 2020

I need to figure out if I'm ready to date. Or to be friends with another man. A friend asked me if I was still thinking about joining my app. I'm leery about a creepy guy coming to the house. He said to stay away because I don't need any weirdo showing up at my door. I'm not sure how to find somebody just to go to dinner with.

Zoosk

July 10th, 2020

I signed up for Zoosk last night. It's a dating site. It's strange because I recognized a couple of guys. I don't know if I'd meet up with somebody yet. I'm worried about what others are going to say. I know I have to do what makes sense to make me happy, but I also don't want to hurt others. They'll always love Steve and the marriage and life we had. It made me who I am today. I think I'm going to put some other information about myself on my page and see what happens. If no one chats, then I know. If someone chats, then I can decide. I am in control. It's all my choice.

Trust?

July 11th, 2020

I deleted the app. I'm too leery that the guys are going to be creepy even though a part of me like the people looked at my profile. One guy messaged me but he smoked. It's so hard to know how trusting I should be or if I should be friends with somebody. I don't want to be with someone that is just looking for a hookup.

Hopeful

July 12th, 2020

In one of the widow groups, a lady said she and a friend have been friends for 20 years and since her husband died the friend has called her every night and now she wonders if there are more than feelings. I told her I was hopeful for her. I'm hopeful for me too. It's hard to know why you feel something. Are you lonely or is it missing the comfort? I'm still wondering if I should move forward. I think it's going to be hard in a small town where everybody knows everyone and everybody knows Steve. But when I'm ready that's what's going to be for me to decide and no one else.

Meeting Someone

July 13th, 2020

I want to meet or chat with somebody but I'm so nervous about sharing too much and them being a predator or them hurting me. Obviously the first time you meet up with somebody I would go in a separate vehicle and somewhere in public. I'm okay with seeing somebody. I know it's okay with Steve. I know what others think shouldn't and doesn't matter. I'll be friends before anything in person or becoming physical. I think I might need to see if a couple friends know anybody that they know who would want to chat with me.

Creating a Profile

July 15th, 2020

I created a profile on Facebook Dating. Who knew it was a thing? It just appeared one day on my facebook page. I really don't know much about it, but you can select to view friends or not. I selected to not view friends but did allow friends of friends which might be nice.

  I had a guy chat with me until I said that I wouldn't meet him until I knew him a little better. He stopped the chat. I guess he just wanted to hook up and I am not ready for that. Who knows if I will ever be ready to be physical with someone? It has to be weird. Even dating seems weird. I think it's hard when it's been so long. I remember being nervous on my first date with Steve even though we were already good friends and had hung out a lot.

Facebook Dating

July 14th, 2020

I started the Facebook dating app today. I've had a few likes and I've deleted those that are too young that live too far away that smoke or are atheist. One guy matched with me but his name was weird. He said that his name was backwards. It was a red flag. He wanted to meet already and I said not yet. I unmatched and blocked him.

Telling the kids

July 1th, 2020

I initially struggled with how to tell my boys and when I did finally tell them that I was thinking of joining a dating app, they all laughed at my choice of app. They didn't seem phased by the news. They think Facebook Dating is for old people. I guess I should be happy they don't think I'm old. I don't feel that 45 is old. They told me that I am not allowed to use Tinder because it is designed for hookups. I am glad they are okay with me moving forward.

I think they are old enough to know this person will not replace their dad but also see that I need someone in my life too. I believe they understand that this person will never, ever, no matter what happens, replace the love I had for Steve and the love he had for us.

I now have to decide how to tell my family and Steve's family. I know that no matter how they find out there is the possibility that they are not going to be ready for me to move forward but I also know that they want me to be happy and right now this is what's making me happy.

Understand My Connections

July 18th, 2020

I've been chatting with a guy through the Facebook dating app. We were talking about religion and the fact that I was going to my in-laws. I want to be honest. I don't want to get involved with somebody who isn't going to understand my connections to my boys, my faith, my family, my job and my hometown. That's who I am. I'm not going to mislead someone and hope that they are not misleading me either. I don't know how I feel about the long distance part. I don't know how about having a new person in my house even for dinner or to watch a movie. This was our space and is also the boys' space.

Driving a Car

July 20th, 2020

I read something today that says grief is like driving a car:

    You can't move forward if you're only using your rear view mirror.

    It's okay to look back to see how far you've come once in a while.

    You need to be focused on the road ahead of you.

    The path you have traveled on has brought you here.

The First Connection

July 22st, 2020

I have been talking with a guy from Minnesota named Mark. We started texting today instead of only going through the app. It's way easier. We talked a little about grief today. He lost his dad a few years ago but is close to his mom. He's really easy to talk to. It's great to have someone to talk with that doesn't already know my story.

Single or Widow?

July 23, 2020

A friend of mine changed his Facebook status to single and it made me think about mine. Do I change it because it's listed as married to Steve? It's linked to our accounts. It makes me wonder about memorializing his account so I can be listed as a widow. I don't think I'm ready to be single because I feel that that makes my marriage seem less or something.

I am glad I joined the Widows Dating after Loss Facebook group. It's helping and encouraging to see that others have found chapter two. Everyone says that each relationship is just different, but it's okay to take it slow and be in control of how it goes. I worry about what people are going to say or think. I know that only people that should get any say in it are my boys. And I think they'd be okay with it because I'm going slow and not just picking-up some creepy guy at the bar. I'd love to have conversations and go to dinner or car rides and to have somebody want to be with me, somebody to hold me when I'm sad.

Chatting

July 27th, 2020

I started chatting with a guy from Facebook Dating today. He seems nice, and I figure that if he turns out to be creepy, there will be a few people to hunt him down. I know that if anyone hurts me that they will have to answer to a lot of people. The funny thing is that I would include Steve on that list if he were still here. I know he wouldn't want to see me get hurt.

This guy is from Minnesota. I'm not sure if a long-distance thing would work, but right now we are just having a conversation. Long distance could be a barrier especially when I work full time and am a mom to three kids and that is only my side of the relationship. He would have time constraints too.

We chatted about grief a little bit. He doesn't have the experience with grief that I do, but he did lose his dad. I have to believe there are similar elements. It is still a loss of a person, the experiences with that person, of having memories and things that cause a burst of grief.

I talked to Mark a little tonight about Steve's death and my tattoo. He told me that it was a neat way to honor him. He also said that he believes in after afterlife and that he knows I will be reunited with Steve someday. I agreed with him.

I then told him that I was worried about dating and falling for someone else. I admitted that I don't know how to do it and I worry about being intimate with someone. I told him how I'm very emotional and I'm afraid I'll fall apart, but that I am working on my confidence. "I want to try it. It will be three years in December. I've done a lot of healing work and counseling." He told me that he was sure that Steve would want me to start dating again and I agreed with him about that too.

Grief is awful, but I believe that death is part of God's plan. I have grown a lot during the past two and half years as I've begun to accept who I am. I am learning how to be a single parent and to run a household on my own. I am learning to trust my intuition and go with what I feel is right for me.

Honesty

August 4th, 2020

I was honest today with Mark. I told him that a friend and I started chatting almost a year ago. We have been friends for a long time, but the tone of our messages has been changing. He's going through a lot right now and says he doesn't want to do long-distance, but I feel there might be something between us. I don't know what I am ready for in a relationship or if I should even be chatting with either of them. I don't want to lead anyone on. When I told Mark, he appreciated my honesty and said that it was hard with his ex being from my area and that there were no hard feelings. We are planning to stay friends. It's nice to have someone else who is looking to date. I can ask him for advice and he shares his experiences.

Not Forgetting

August 14th, 2020

Today I wrote a blog post using information from the introduction of this memoir. I then shared it with my family and Seve's family as my way of letting them know about my decision to start dating.

I am moving forward but I am not forgetting. I am ready for new love and maybe a person to be my chapter two.

I have mixed feelings about how this will go but I am also excited about the possibilities.

I sent a message to Jim. He's supposed to be in the area working on a friend's floor in my area. We've been chatting for a couple of days through one of the dating apps. In my message, I asked, "Is it too early or weird if I asked if you want to grab food while you're in town? I'm so new to this that I don't know what's appropriate or not. Last time I went on a date was when I was 16." I told him that I wanted to meet somewhere in public and then I would meet him there. He said that that sounded good and smart. Then he asked if he could tell me that he liked my eyes without it sounding like he was hitting on me.

We're going to meet around noon on Wednesday to go for lunch.

Am I crazy or insane or just ready? What about the fact that I haven't told any of my family or Steve's family that I'm even thinking of meeting someone or joining dating apps and now I just agreed to meet someone in public. So excited and nervous at the same time.

Responses

August 14-15th, 2021

I spent way too much time and effort being worried about what others would think or say or feel. Everyone is super supportive and okay with my decision...I don't know why I expected a different reaction. I need to just do what is best for me and then let others decide their feelings. I am happy that others are okay with it. I find it funny that it seems like a lot of them have been talking about it before I even said anything.

From Steve's dad:

" As I sit here with tears running down my face we want you to know we also want you to be happy. Steve WOULD want you to be happy. "

From Steve's sister:

" I support you in whatever steps you are ready to take. It makes me happy that you have come to a place where you can think of love again. You are a beautiful and amazing woman. I won't lie. It may be hard and strange to see you enter the dating world and enter into a relationship if anything should happen, but it is also something I deeply wish for you. Your spirit is too beautiful to purposefully close it off to the possibility of love again. Carrying Steve with you is different than putting him as an insurmountable wall around you. Just know that I love you, my sister. "

From Steve's mom:

"We love you Em and we want you to be happy. I talked to Rick (my dad) quite some time ago and I said you're a beautiful young woman and I felt when the time was right you would find someone. We did agree that when you found the right one Rick will have to have the - she's my daughter and I love her and you better treat her right because I have 280 acres and a shovel - talk. We love you.

From my mom to Steve's parents and sister:

Just always remember who are forever family!

From my sister:

I am proud of you, both for getting to this point and being brave enough to act on it and for telling everyone. You're one of the strongest people I've ever met. Can't wait to hear how the date goes.

From my mom:

Read your blog. I love you honey and always want your happiness.

From my Aunt Karen:

Totally, completely agree, moving forward! Beautifully written!! You make me proud. Thank you for sharing it with me. So you really did a dating app?

I saw Stacy last night and then went out to the camp. I saw mom, dad, my sister and brother-in-law. Everybody seems okay with it. BMy sister and her husband had bets placed that I would start dating again and she thought I would, so she won. My dad asked if I had a specific person that he needed to warn about the property. The warning is that he has a lot of property and a shovel if anyone was to hurt me.

 I don't know about being the strongest person. I just feel ready. I think all of the conversations I had with the other two men helped me get to this point. To know that they both thought I was attractive and knowing my story was interesting.

 I am excited to meet up with Jim. He seems really nice. We have already had some good conversations. Really nervous about what to say and how long to be at the restaurant. I am glad I am taking my own car so if it is weird I can leave.

Proud of Me

August 16th, 2020

I'm hurt that I thought something was starting. It's okay because it was a lesson from God saying that he wasn't the one. While I was waiting I felt so excited and a little nervous but also a few tears started. It's a big step to move forward but I feel that Steve was watching me and that he wants me to be happy. Since I can't be with him anymore I need to find love here on earth. I'll never not love Steve. I'll always want to be with him. I loved our marriage and our relationship. I still miss him so much. I miss the love, the touch, his sense of humor, having coffee together and going for rides. I miss his faith and us going to church together. I miss helping him get his classroom together. I miss his support and caring. I miss being able to share things.

This ironically is something that I want to share with him. To hear what he thinks about the guys or the distance or if they're creepy or a scam. Maybe my fears yesterday were a sign that this wasn't going to work out. He knew this wasn't a thing. I think Steve's proud of who I've grown into, how I am more confident, moving forward, more willing to be honest, and seeing myself as beautiful.

Excited but Tears Too

August 19th, 2020

Me: I'm supposed to meet Jim this afternoon for lunch. I feel kind of beautiful and excited, but tears are starting too.

    Friend: Don't be nervous. You'll be just fine. It's just a date. You can feel him out a bit and see how you feel after today. It's a big step but you'll be okay.

    Fast forward a few hours…I was stood up. I can't believe he just ghosted me. I can see that he has been on the app but has not responded to any of my messages. It's so unlike him. We have been chatting back and forth throughout the past many days. I assume he got nervous, but he really could send a message back saying he changed his mind or something so I am not left wondering. I feel hurt and upset. I guess I put a lot of pressure on myself that the first guy I sort of connected with would want to meet up. Maybe it was just too early.

"Match"

August 22nd, 2020

I joined the Match app, but so far no response is to any of my chats. I don't know how to know if people are paying and not responding or if they only have the free version to see what's out there before making a commitment. $80 for 3 months but I'm serious so I'm going to try it. I'm not sure if I'd continue Zoosks. The view profile thing bugs me because I think it just pops up even though they're not really viewing my profile.

    I had prayed for things to go well with Jim and maybe God's idea of well was it for it to end. I can't help but think he was lying to me and couldn't keep that up and didn't want to hurt me. I also think he showed up and felt that I chickened out but I didn't. He obviously didn't read my text. Who knows? I'm trying not to be bothered but I feel that he was disrespectful.

New Guy

August 27th, 2020

I have been chatting with a new guy, Donnie, and he just sent a message that he has to work this weekend. He's going to check and see about next weekend. I am not sure what is going to happen. I worry about the long distance piece. I already struggle with finding time for me, for the kids, for family and for work stuff. We have connected a lot because of grief. He has lost quite a few people recently. Many were sudden and unexpected. He has kids so he understands the parenting part of dating.

Unconditional Love

August 28th, 2020

I think I have gotten to a place where I realize that worrying is useless and I'm so confident in God's plan, that I worry so much less. Surviving grief and realizing how much losing Steve has forced me and allowed me to grow as a person and as a mom proves to me that God was right. I know He always is but to accept that He knew what He was doing, feels incredible. To accept Steve's death, to know he's in heaven, to know that God knew I could be without Steve and be okay, and to feel good, is amazing.

God granted me him for 25 years in a relationship, longer if you count being classmates and friends. He knew that was long enough to learn about unconditional love from a non-family member, to become a mom, to understand marriage, to grow in my faith, to learn the hard way about honesty and budgeting, to learn what being a partner involves and to know and feel loved and wanted.

Since Steve died, I've also learned that my faith was what was most important. Without it, I couldn't have loved, been a mom or a wife and our marriage wouldn't have been as strong. My trust in God allowed me to grieve, to be sad, depressed, anxious, overwhelmed, angry, hurt, confused, scared, and at the same time so happy and blessed to have had him. My faith allowed me to be okay some days, to get out of bed, comfort others, believe in myself, increase my confidence, be still, ask questions and be okay not getting the answers, and know that I'm loved no matter who is in this physical world or watching us from in heaven.

Through prayer and journaling, meditation and healing, through myofascial release, and through counseling, I worked with my faith, my body, my soul, my mind, and my spirit to allow peace to enter, to use my strength to find joy, and allow myself to feel happy, good, okay and to accept that whatever I feel is what is meant to be. I'm allowed to be okay and not okay at the same time.

There's no wrong in grief. No specified rules. No timelines. No book to say what to do or how to do it. We each just need to travel to joy on our own and accept help and healing along the way. Our loved ones would want us to be happy. They did when they were here. That hasn't changed because their bodies aren't here and we don't get to go for a long car ride with them.

The signs Steve gave me; leaving quarters, moving the shower curtain to touch my leg, and a fruit fly in a strange place, all were saying, "You've got this". "You're good". "Suck it up buttercup". "I'll always love you". "Be happy".

Moving forward, I know I need to make decisions for myself based on what's right for me. I should have always been doing this but I didn't. I always wanted everyone to be happy and at peace and I still do but I also now want that for myself and realize it's not separate. I can be happy and others can be happy at the same time even if they don't trust my choices.

Another Widow?

August 31st, 2020

Today I am wondering if I should look for a widower. It would be nice to have someone that gets losing your spouse. It is such a different kind of loss from that of a grandparent, an aunt or a friend. I think I want someone who understands the grief part of my life.

I also wonder about kids. I am not opposed to someone having children. I think the scheduling part would be hard. I already have a hard time doing things around my kids' schedule and I wonder if I am spending enough time with them. I am thankful they are the ages they are and not teeny. They can be left home for the evening and it's not a big deal.

Self-doubt again today. I'm ready to move forward, but I'm doubtful that anyone will want to meet me. I've been ghosted twice and have not had any other matches. I think being a widow and too tall from a small town might all be working against me. I might try changing my status in the apps to "single" instead of "widow". Maybe that term is intimidating. It can be something I share once I get to know someone a little better.

Steve's Wishes

September 1st, 2020

I believe that Steve would want me to be happy, but I wish I remembered him saying it to me. I wish I knew we'd talked about it. Even if it hurts him he's not here anymore. Can you be hurt once you're in heaven? Can you feel pain? Does your heart break? I assume not. I assume you can see the joy and the love in every situation. I imagine you just want others to be at peace and experience a life God has given to each person. I imagine Steve wants me to live my life, but to be careful. To not get hurt. To not sacrifice family or the boys to be with somebody, anybody. We were starting to focus more on us before he died as the boys had gotten older but their needs still came first.

We knew we needed our marriage to be strong and to build love and our relationship though to be able to be good parents and role models for the boys. I worry that I'm too honest and too confident there's a phrase I never thought I'd say! I worry about my height being a turn off. I worry I'm too overweight. I worry my likes and interests are too boring. I worry because I don't like outdoor activities or motorcycles or fishing or sports. I worry I share too much so there's nothing for someone to learn about me.

Dear God,

Help me to not worry. Help me to see your love and feel your plan and purpose for my life. Help me continue to help others on their journey. Help someone find me and know that they'll like to know more. Help me do what's right for me and the boys. Help me continue to be confident and to be at peace. continue to bless me with miracles, love, hope, faith and peace. Thank you for strength, peace, joy and confidence. Thank you for being the constant in the ever-changing world. Thank you for the past that's allowed me to grow. Thank you for the present where I live with you and me. Thank you for the hope of eternal life in my future.

Amen

Ghosted Again!

September 4th, 2020

Unbelievable! I got ghosted again. I asked Donnie why he wouldn't consider me coming there or if he wanted to wait until the 12th. No response. Gone. Why can someone not have the decency to message someone? Even just a, "Hey. I can't do this right now" or "I changed my mind". Or better yet, be honest and say, "you were moving too fast" or "I have been lying to you this whole time and can't do it anymore." I thought we had a connection with the grief piece. I thought I had found out enough about him to verify what he was saying. I felt attraction and thought he did too. I wonder if it is me? Do people really not want to date a widow? Maybe my looks although they clicked on my profile and could see multiple pictures. Is it because I have kids? I don't know how much more I want to try these apps. I think I might just wait and see if someone I know knows someone. The lesson I have learned is that I am ready to meet someone.

Dating, Yet Missing

September 12th, 2020

I still want to date someone, maybe something casual and I am not sure about the long-term relationship and not wanting a friend with benefits or a one-night stand. I definitely don't want to be involved with an open marriage or by someone already involved or married. I miss being hugged and cuddling in the mornings. I miss feeling loved. Maybe missing isn't enough to have somebody match with me and be serious.

Do You Pick Agates?

September 13th, 2020

You know how on facebook notifications, it lets you know who likes your posts? I keep seeing a guy named Chris liking my photography. I wasn't sure who he was or why we were friends. Then I realized that I know his older sister and we were on the swim team together in high school. I also know one of his other sisters from church. Hmmm. A local guy whose family I know. I decided to reach out to him through messenger.

" I saw you liked my agates picture. Thanks! Do you search for them too?"
"That was a cool pic. I usually find cool colored rocks. I never had any luck finding agates."
"We could go to the beach like Calumet Waterworks and I could try to teach you if you want to sometime."
"I think it would be fun to know how to find them. Let me know sometime when you're going."
"We could go next weekend. I am always up for going to the beach"

"Sounds good"

"I have something at 4:30 on Saturday but we could go before that. It's usually not very sunny until around noon"

"I can meet you at Calumet Waterworks at 12:00 on Saturday if that works."

"Sounds good."

I am super excited and a little overwhelmed that I just made plans to meet someone. I am nervous and excited. I wonder if this counts as a date???? Do I want it to be a date?

Let's Talk About the Weather

September 17th, 2020

"Looks like the weather is going to be good on Saturday", he messages. I respond with, "Looks like sunshine!"

I am not sure what to wear. What do I talk about? Is it going to be awkward? What will he think about me? Do you think he'll be attracted? Do I want that? I am really ready to date. I really don't feel he is going to ghost me like the others.

My mom is excited that I am meeting someone local. I think she feels that means he's not a murderer.

Cool?

September 17th, 2020

I messaged Chris about looking forward to Saturday. His response was "cool". I'm not sure what that means. Does it mean that he is okay with meeting but not looking forward to it or does he just not text?

I had a guy from the local area like me through the Facebook dating app today I messaged him back. I'm not sure how any of this works.

I talked a little bit to a friend about my worries about intimacy. She said she's only dated two people, her ex and her husband and that is different with each person.

I really miss being hugged and curling up with somebody to watch a movie.

Morning Thoughts

September 19th, 2020

2 years and 9 months.

I woke up wishing that I could have been laying next to Steve with my hand on his chest. Maybe because I'm meeting Chris by the beach today to hopefully show him how to find agates. I hope it turns into something.

I know his family. I was probably at his childhood home when I was a junior in high school. He's local, which is helpful for getting together. I don't feel nervous about meeting him but it's weird because I don't really know him at all. No idea even how old he is. I know somewhere around my age based on his sister's ages. I do wonder what if we have nothing in common? What if he smokes or smells? What if he ghosts me like the other people? I am going to be heartbroken if he is not there.

First Date

September 19th, 2020

I didn't need to worry so much! He was there already when I pulled up. We spent three hours on the beach at Calumet Works today walking, talking and him learning to find agates. We were both hungry and ended the day with pizza at Nutini's. It was nice to have someone to hang out with. He's really kind and pretty good-looking. And I'm not too emotional so I guess that means I am ready. He helped me down from climbing over a tree, he put his hand on my back another time and we ended the day with a hug. I think it was a date.

I wasn't sure going into today. I am really excited! I feel connected already. He messaged me saying that he had a really good time and he gave me his number.

I am sure I talked too much and I brought up Steve a couple of times. He played hockey with Steve when they were little. So many connections in our past. I am sure we are meant to know each other. I am not sure how we could have gone to the same school and church and not remembered each other. I guess because he was two years behind me and very quiet. So excited! I can hardly sleep and I can not stop smiling!

I told him that I hoped I didn't talk too much about Steve and his death. He told me I "didn't and I want you to know it's all good."

We then texted about Tuesday. He asked what we should do and I responded with dinner and sunset. His answer was "It's a date". I am feeling like a high schooler…nervous and excited. I am going on a date!!!!

Love Already

September 21st, 2020

I may be feeling love already. How can that be? One date, but it was awesome. I felt so comfortable. I felt taken care of and we were only walking on the beach. I messaged last night with a picture of the sunset and said I wished that he were there. Brave? Crazy? Too fast too much? But he responded with a cool picture and said "I will be on Tuesday".

I woke up yesterday and today thinking about him. I put gum in my purse so after we eat I can chew gum in case he tries to kiss me. Can I hope? I offered to pick him up and he said sure. I looked at where his house was last night but it was really dark.

My sister knows all three of his sisters. She said his brother is the husband of my parapro from my classroom when I was teaching. He's the baby of the family of five. I feel so right to be with him. I didn't think about looks or height or anything but he helped me over a tree and said I got you. Then he rubbed my back a little bit at a later point. We hugged at the end of dinner.

Giddy

September 22nd, 2020

I messaged my Aunt Karen today: "When you said the other day that you felt giddy, that's exactly how I feel. I am picking up Chris and we're going to dinner and then going to watch the sunset. I am beyond excited. I am struggling to get work done because I keep thinking about it."

I feel excited for today. I made a bag up for the beach with a blanket, gummy bears, Hershey Kisses, water and an Arnold Palmer for him and a Vitamin Water for me. I'm not sure we'll need any of it but just in case he wants to sit and watch the sunset with his arm around me and then lean in for a kiss. Ugh? Am I right or okay thinking about him kissing me on the second date? I don't think it's because I miss physical touch. I think it's because I'm attracted to him. He has such a cute smile, dark hair and a short beard. I guess he's my height because I didn't notice it. I like the way he helped me on the beach. He hugged me back at the end of our date. He said his ex didn't like to hold hands or hug or kiss and that's one of the reasons he ended it.

I wonder who he has told and if he's excited too or if guys don't get that way?

I think I'll be heartbroken if this doesn't work out after 5 hours together. Is that crazy or meant to be? Facebook usually shows how long you've been friends and it doesn't show our friendship date. I have no idea when or who the friendship started with. It's cool how I noticed that he started liking my post. I'm so thankful for God working through us to bring us together. I want to know if he likes me and if he thinks I'm pretty and if he wants to kiss me.

Dating

September 23rd, 2020

My date last night went really well. We went to dinner and then sat on the beach to watch the sunset and the stars. At one point he was looking at me instead of the sunset. He told me it was because I was pretty. I knew he was going to kiss me and I let it happen. It felt more good than weird but I did end up pulling away a little bit. A few tears fell. I apologized and he told me that I just need to take it at my own pace and that he is not in any hurry. I told him that it was a little weird and he said that was understandable. We kissed a couple more times after that. We're planning to get together again tomorrow and maybe over the weekend depending on the weather. It feels easy and natural.

    I told him about my tattoo and what it meant. The tattoo is a circle traced from Steve's wedding ring with the word love in the center in his handwriting over my heart. I showed him a picture of it. He seemed okay with that too. He said everyone has a past.

    He said he's thankful that he dated a girl last year because it gave him the courage to go out with me. He's a pretty quiet guy. I guess he always has been. He always felt he was going to be single and not have a connection to anyone. He's really easy to be around and makes me feel super comfortable. I feel like I'm a high school teenager again. I even had trouble falling asleep last night!

I'm pretty positive God is making this happen. Neither of us can remember becoming facebook friends. I think it's weird how I started noticing that he liked my posts. I feel very comfortable around him and it's just easy.

Matthew told me that he is glad to see me excited because it's been a long time.

Not in a Hurry

September 24th, 2020

I'm so excited and happy. A little bit of tears and being upset right now. I still wish Steve were here and I wasn't doing this but I know he's not. He's not coming back and I have the right to be happy.

We're planning to get together again tomorrow. He said we can do whatever I want and that he likes buying me dinner.

Is Dating Really Okay?

September 25th, 2020

I'm super excited...a little like a high schooler starting to date but every now and then I wonder if it is okay. It's weird being with someone but also feels right with him.

Messaged a friend today: "Today's a questioning day. Wondering if dating is okay and I know it's all in my head but still teary today. Then I feel dumb because it's not like I'm cheating or that Steve's coming back. I'm an adult."

His response was, " Yes, dating is okay. I know it's weird because ultimately it could be a new chapter in the long run, but just take it slowly and see where it goes. That's all you can do. It'll start feeling better as time goes on."

My Aunt Karen told me, "You're a strong woman. Steve helped make you who you are today and that is something any good man moving forward will appreciate."

I think I will stop by his house and see if he is around. We are supposed to watch a movie at his house tonight.

Facebook Status

September 25th, 2020

When I got home last night, Chris had changed his status on Facebook to "in a relationship". I wasn't sure what I wanted to do. I debated if it was the right time for me and decided that what we have is a relationship so I changed my status too. I told him that it was a little weird to remove the word 'widow' but that I was excited. He told me that he thought maybe he should have talked to me before he changed it. I'm planning to spend more time with him tonight. Things are moving quickly but I feel like I am in a good place. He is letting me set the pace. I went through all kinds of emotions, from tears to excitement to confusion and back to excitement. Choosing the excitement path. Feeling all the feels. I texted him and said, "I changed my status too. Mixed emotions: it was hard to remove 'widow' from my status but I'm excited about what we have."

My mom is worried that it is all happening too quickly. But she does seem happy for me.

I talked with my Aunt Karen about Steve and all of this. We both agree that my relationship with him will shape my relationship with Chris. I realize that the time I had with Steve was what I needed even if it was hard. She said that Steve helped make me who I am today and that is something that any good man going forward will appreciate.

Meeting My Kids

September 26th, 2020

I spent the afternoon with Chris at his house and then he came over to my house to meet the kids. Michael said he seemed like a normal guy and seemed nice. They gabbed about cars for a while. Skylar said he seems perfect for me. Matthew only kind of introduced himself and then went back upstairs to game. Brian wasn't around so they didn't get to meet. We ate some pizza and then watched TV. He actually fell asleep for a little bit. He stayed until almost midnight.

It felt okay to have him at my house but I feel a little more comfortable at his. I wasn't sure with it being the house that Steve and I lived in together. I guess there is not a lot of Steve's stuff around anymore.

Sorry, I'm in a Relationship

September 26th, 2020

Even though I made the fb dating app inactive, a guy reached out today and asked me out. I had chatted with this guy a couple of weeks before I met Chris. I told him, "I'm sorry I'm in a relationship." I also explained that I thought the app was inactive. It's awesome to be able to say I am in a relationship.

Happy Having You in My Life

September 27th, 2020

He told me today that he is really happy to have me in his life. He talked about his ex a little bit and how their relationship was very different. I love that we can be honest with each other about our pasts. It would be really hard to be in a relationship and not be able to talk about Steve...he was part of my life for 25 years. I appreciate that Chris lets me share stories and memories. I also love how kind and sweet he is when I am having a hard time or a grief moment. He gets it though because he lost both of his parents in the past 10 years.

Connected

September 28th, 2020

I'm already feeling super connected to him and wanting to spend time with him all the time. I hope I didn't scare him away by having him meet the boys in Skylar. I worry that I'm moving too quickly and falling too fast. How can you fall in love in a week? He's such a good guy.

Parenting

September 29th, 2020

I am torn between being with Chris and being a responsible parent. How much time do I spend with each of them? I think I worry that my kids will miss me if I am not home but then again they are often in their rooms playing games and probably wouldn't even know I wasn't home.

I'm not worrying about what anybody else thinks but I do want my boys to be okay with him and the fact that I'm starting a relationship with someone. I think because they're older and know that this guy is not coming in to try to be a dad or replace Steve makes it easier. Most of the people that have heard that I am in a relationship or saw it on Facebook have been really happy for me.

Longer then 2 Weeks

October 1st, 2020

It is so nice to have someone to hold hands with and cuddle while watching TV. We have quite a few of the same interests. His sister messaged me a picture from the summer and said that she is so happy that he has found someone. It hasn't even been two weeks and yet I feel like it has been longer. We've really connected. People have been commenting that our smiles are the same in the selfie that I took of us.

Triggered

October 4th, 2020

Weird how a smell can be such a trigger. I smelled the body wash that Chris has and it instantly made me cry. I used to spread Steve's body wash on the shower walls and cry as my way of grieving. I felt that no one could hear me if I played music loudly and sobbed in the shower. My body today associated that smell with grief.

Chris was really understanding and said he would get different soap for at his house. I just love that he hugs me and lets me cry. He told me I can express my emotions anytime.

Almost "I Love You"

October 5th, 2020

I almost said I love you a couple of times. I don't want to freak him out. But I think he feels the same. I thought about marriage after Matthew graduates but also about living with him and what I sell this house? Who knows? What happens with Steve's retirement money if I was to get remarried? I know the death benefits and I know I'll still get my full retirement.

Missing Him

October 6th, 2020

I am not sure if I will see Chris today or not. I'm waiting to see if he will invite me over. We are planning a date on Thursday. I know he won't forget about me if I don't see him for a day, but I miss him.

Falling for You

October 7th, 2020

I told Chris Monday night that I think I'm falling for him. He said no one's ever told him that before. We watch the sunset together. He met my mom, dad and sister for a few minutes. My sister said it was only fair since we know his family that he gets to know mine.

I've been having thoughts about Chris being at Michael and Skylar's wedding. There may be an empty chair on one side of me to honor Steve. It's going to be really hard to not have them there to celebrate such a huge event. I keep wondering if the kids will have any scripture readings. I wish I could read 1st Corinthians for them but think I'd be way too emotional.

I've been talking with my Aunt Karen quite a bit. It seems funny her asking me for advice but I'm happy to be able to help guide others through all parts of this grief journey: the heartbreak, the sour, the crazies, and the new love. God put me here at this time in history to be a teacher of Steve and our marriage of the boys as a parent, the hundreds of kids at school and church and two widows on this journey.

God,

Thank you for your faith and trust in me to fulfill your purpose to be able to grieve and to love at the same time, to experience the Holy Spirit and miracles. Help me heal from anger and her. Help others be able to experience joy through your love.

Amen.

Choices

October 12th, 2020

A friend of mine has split custody with his ex wife and we were talking about how kids can throw a wrench into a new relationship but that we wouldn't change having kids. I told him that it is sometimes hard because Chris never had children but that he is super understanding of me being a mom. I need to remember that because he wasn't married and doesn't have children that I need to also be understanding and sometimes explain things that I am doing or feeling related to being a mom. It's hard to navigate being a single mom in a new relationship.

Questioning Things

October 16th, 2020

Last night I was crying and talked quite a bit to Chris. I told him how unsure I was about everything related to dating and being with a new person. He comforted me and we're still good. He reminded me that he has never been in a real relationship and this is all new to him too. He didn't kick me out for crying, so I guess that's a good thing. I shouldn't have been worried at all, he's never been anything but caring and kind. I wish I had more confidence in myself to share my thoughts and feelings instead of letting them build up.

Choosing Me

October 17th, 2020

"Thank you again for hugging and holding me, saying I'm beautiful and keeping me."

"You're welcome. It was my pleasure. I was showing you how much I care for you. I am lucky to have met such a great girl. Thanks for choosing me Emilie."

"I am going to choose you every day".

I ended the texts today by saying "I love you". I am not sure I ever thought I would say those words again after losing Steve but it's easy with Chris.

In response to someone asking how I am, I answered, "In Love". So amazing to feel this way!

Worried About Nothing

October 18th, 2020

I woke up last night worried that maybe I am moving too quickly. When I told Chris about it he was really understanding and loving. He held me while I cried and told me that he cares a lot about me. I realize that I don't really compare my relationship with Chris to my relationship with Steve. There have been a couple times that it really hit me. I am happy. I know that I will never forget Steve and our love and marriage but Chris knows that and is supportive. I'm in a good place!

One Month Already

October 19th, 2020

One month with Chris.

2 years and 10 months without Steve.

I'm okay with both. I loved our marriage and story. I love who I've become through my grief journey. I love who I am when I'm with Chris. Thank you to God for bringing two men into my life who love me and care for me. I wish this love too for my boys. Chris said he loved me too. He worries about me and doing what's right.

I texted him about how often he wants to see me this week because I don't want to wear out my welcome but he said he's fine seeing me everyday and that I'm always welcome.

Being Together

October 21st, 2020

I talked with Chris about past relationships. He talked about his ex and how that relationship hurt his self confidence. Is it weird that I am a little bit glad he has some difficulty in his past too? Not that I want him to be hurt, but now I can focus on helping him heal and move forward and not worry about myself as much.

I messaged Chris, "I love spending time with you and how comfortable you make me feel. I'm not going anywhere. I don't want you to be upset with anything we do. I'm not your ex but I know how hard dealing with the past can be. I really struggle to feel loveable and sexy but you make me feel both."

He wrote back with this: "You are so beautiful and I love your body's curves. I want to make good memories with you and forget my old ones. I'm happy to have you in my life."

Article

November 4th, 2020

Shared an article today with Chris about how to tell if this time it's going to be worth it. There were eight signs to look for in a relationship. We met all eight of them. "That's good to hear" was his response. I told him, I knew he was a keeper before I read the article. He is incredible. I feel so blessed to be with someone who is so caring and loving. I shouldn't be surprised because I chose that with Steve too.

Things in Common

November 11th, 2020

I see Chris almost every day and we have been making meals together. We're planning things for the spring and summer when the weather gets nice. He would like to show me some waterfalls that I have never been to before. It is wonderful to have someone to do things with and for us to have common interests like photography, sunsets, waterfalls and watching game shows on TV. I love thinking about us being together in the summer. It's fun to think about the future and knowing that he will be a part of it.

Thank You

November 14th, 2020

Dear Lord, Thank you for a second chance at love. It has been so easy to feel loved by Chris and I need that. Amen.

Ill

November 24th, 2020

I have been sick for over a week already. I have a fever/chills, body aches and a horrible cough. Chris has done a great job of taking care of me. I spent the last two days with him and he is making me food and getting me what I need so I don't have to move a lot. Even getting up to go to the bathroom still takes so much energy and makes me cough. I can tell he is worried about me. When I thank him, he says that's what he is there for.

   I realized that being apart for the week was hard. I was getting used to seeing him at least every other day. It was strange to not cuddle and watch TV with him. Phone calls are different and not as personal. It has been great being together. It shows me that our relationship is strong.

Missing Steve

December 15th, 2020

Last night I was thinking about how it will be 3 years on Saturday and how much I miss Steve. I felt bad because I was with Chris, but thinking about Steve. Chris questioned my crying and asked if I still wanted to be with him. I absolutely assured him that I wanted to be with him but that I felt weird. He told me that it is okay to miss Steve and that because he left me suddenly I have a lot of responsibilities but I'm doing a good job. He just held me and let me cry.

I messaged him this morning that I definitely did not want it to end and that I loved having him in my life. He wrote this back:

"I'm always here if you need me. I'm happy having you in my life. I'm glad you don't want it to end. I'm with you and I am not going anywhere."

He's going to come to my house for Christmas dinner. He originally said he wasn't sure because he wanted to do what I was comfortable with. I told him that I wanted him to be comfortable too. We agreed that dinner would be okay even with Steve's parents and Stacy coming too. They want to meet him and have offered to have him at their house.

I feel so blessed to have Steve's family as a part of my life and supportive of my relationship with Chris. I know they want me to be happy.

3 Years and also 3 Months

December 19th, 2020

Three years since Steve died.

Three years since my first date with Chris.

It's weird how time works. In some ways, it seems like Steve has been gone for so long and in other ways, I feel like I saw him yesterday. It's been 3 years since he left this earth and started watching over us.

It seems like we've gotten a grip on the new normal... not having him at dinner, not making him coffee in the morning, not getting any hugs, making decisions on my own, and being okay without him here.

My new normal now includes a new person as well. It's been 3 months since I started seeing someone. I spent a lot of time this past week feeling weird. I was in a space where I wanted to be with Chris but also really missing Steve. I know Steve and I would still be together if he hadn't died. I also know that Steve wouldn't want me to be alone. Chris told me that it is okay to be sad and to miss him.

I wasn't sure how I was going to spend the three-year anniversary day and wondered if it would be okay to spend it with Chris. It was!

We went and visited his niece at her critter farm. It was something so different than I had spent that day in the past that it made the day easier. I spent the evening with Steve's parents for his dad's birthday dinner.

I feel so blessed that God has given me two men to be in a relationship with. I will never forget the love that Steve and I shared and our marriage. But I'm now learning that I can keep that love and also have a new love.

Christmas Letter

December 2020

Here is part of my annual Christmas letter:

My biggest news this year is starting a relationship with Chris. He liked one of my pictures of agates on Facebook. I asked if he wanted to meet and learn how to pick them and he agreed. I've seen him almost everyday since. He is from Hancock and lives not too far away with his two dogs. We have a lot in common like nature photography and watching movies. I wasn't sure I would be ready to be in a relationship with someone again, but this feels right.

Freckles

December 27th, 2020

Chris has the shape of a seven made out of freckles on his shoulder. I told them that if he had gotten one more dot from a tattoo he could make a triangle. He said he's not sure he'd ever get a tattoo because he doesn't know what he'd get and that he'd have to get something that he'd want to look at for the rest of his life. I felt the same way about getting a tattoo until after Steve died.

Tattoo?

January 4th, 2021

I finally asked Chris if my tattoo bugged him and he said no. I told him that it bugs me sometimes. It does in the sense that I don't want him to think about Steve when we're together and I guess I don't think about Steve as much as I do the tattoo itself. Steve is and always will be my love forever and forever. Tattoos kept coming into conversations and on TV so I knew I needed to talk about it.

Happy 4 Months

January 19th, 2021

My morning text from Chris said. "Good morning. Happy 4 months. Have a good day at work." I'm so glad he sent the message. I'm sure I would have realized it when I wrote the date. I'm very much in love.

Clingy

February 7th, 2021

I also worry that I'm too clingy with Chris. I feel like I do all the planning of what we're going to do and how much time we spend together but it could just be because I'm busy or have kids. I've never told him I want him to plan things or let me know if I'm too much. I think he's pretty honest with me. In fact he's always been honest since the very start. I also think his past relationship was pretty casual. I just don't want him to feel controlled or obligated to spend time every time I suggest it. I want him to do what he needs to do.

Not All the Answers

February 16th, 2021

I love being with Chris. It's hard to think about not seeing him everyday. He told me he likes to have me over and that I'm not a pain. This is only his second long-term relationship so he's learning. It's mine too and I'm learning and I need to remember that neither of us have all the answers. We can learn together and we will make mistakes, but we also need to be honest with each other so we can work through it.

Future

March 11th, 2021

Chris talks about our future. He bought a sauna for us to use. He talks about going to his camp and waterfalls. I don't know that there will ever be more than what we have now. I just really want to be with him. We just fit together. It's exciting to be planning for a future with another person. I'm realizing how much I missed having a partner to do things with and to talk about plans.

What About Marriage?

March 13th, 2021

Chris wants me to be in his future and I want that too, but I wonder about marriage. Is that something he's thought about or is he good just being in a relationship? I don't even know if I'm ready or ever will be. I think I'd love to be married to Chris with a small wedding at a waterfall but I worry about where we'd live and about money. I don't mind sharing but I think he'd feel weird using money as ours. He doesn't like to travel and I don't think he would ever move. I think I want something that would be our place so we are both moving and creating a place for us. I'm pretty sure I'd say yes if he ever proposed. I love him and want to be with him!

I worry that he has been saying he's old and falling apart because of his wrists and shoulders. It reminds me of comments Steve said before he died. I'm going to be terrified if Chris says he has to have surgery because of Steve dying after having routine surgery that supposedly went well. I am not sure I am ready to go through that again so soon.

Going for a Ride

March 17th, 2021

It's so fun to just be with Chris. That we like a lot of the same things. He's so patient with me. He's so loving and doesn't ever want to see me hurting.

Today we took a ride to Copper Harbor. We stopped many times to take pictures and pick rocks. It's great to just be able to go for a ride and hold hands in the car. We talked the whole time…although I am sure I do most of the talking.

What about the Future?

March 19th, 2021

6 months with Chris and I'm so in love.

I see our future together even though I don't know what it's going to look like. Maybe marriage or what we have or living together? A lot of my Facebook memories involved Steve today. I have lots to learn and to trust. I have to accept and know that it's okay to still love Steve and to also love Chris. Steve was here to teach me to be loving and caring and how to be in a relationship and Chris is here for me to learn to love myself first in a relationship.

Dear Lord, Thank you for my life, the gifts, the sorrow, and the love. Thank you for my family and friends for their love, the truth, honesty and forgiveness. Continue to bless me with memories of both Steve and Chris. Amen.

Ring, Proposal, Name

March 20th, 2021

I asked my kids today what they think Chris used his stimulus money for. One of them guessed a ring. I also had a woman at work tell me she wondered when an invitation would come from me and Chris. He was okay with me telling him about both of these situations. He even hinted that maybe after the kids are grown up. (My youngest is only 14.) I don't know if I'm ready to be married again. What about my name? Do I change it again? I guess I'd be retired or doing something else where it wouldn't be in my email address and on my professional signature. I don't know if Chris would want that. I don't know about me living there either, but it would be easier than thinking of him living here. Lots of questions but I need to continue to be honest and that makes all the difference.

Forever

March 31st, 2021

I've been thinking a lot about marriage lately. I don't know what marriage would look like for us or if it even makes sense to do a formal wedding and marriage. I do know that I want to be with him forever. I really need to trust. I need to trust God and that he brought Chris to me.

I See Us Together

April 5th, 2021

I asked my friend, "Do you think that someday I'll be ready to get married?" His response was it depends on my heart and it may change after the kids are grown too. Then we talked about living arrangements. I don't know about us living here and I am also not sure about his house. But I do think Chris and I will stay together. I still find it hard to believe that it's only been six months.

Matthew

April 20th, 2021

I spent a lot of time with Matthew today. Chris told me that Matthew is only young once so I should spend time with him. Chris said that he'll be there when I can be with him.

It was 7 months yesterday, He said seven more then I said 70 or 700 more. 70 more would make us 115 years old. It sounds like he does want to be with me forever. This is something that a couple of years ago I would never have thought I would want. I always pictured growing old with Steve and once that was taken away, I thought I would have to figure out how to be single for the rest of my life.

Each Other

May 8th, 2021

I got the following message from Chris today. I love when he sends longer messages. Usually our texts are just good morning or good night. He told me:

"I love you too. I love doing things with you. I will always be with you. We compliment each other. You're my perfect match."

I got him a rose bush in honor of the memory of his mom. He told me once that he always got a rose bush for Mother's Day. He was very touched by the thought and that I remembered.

Music

May 13th, 2021

I shared the song "Say You Won't Let Go" with Chris after an awesome walk on the beach and watching the sunset together. Lyrics are something like 'I'll love you even when we're old and gray.' We laughed about having gray back hair...both of us. There's also another part about being in love even when we're ghosts and I sure hope that's the case. I hope he's my chapter 2. The next love of my lifetime or his. I really feel I'm meant to love him so he's not alone. His siblings all have spouses and kids and grandkids. His mom and dad are both gone. I don't know how long we have but I'm going to take and have all I can. I know how to grieve. I know how to love. I know how to go on and move forward. Am I ready? I guess so, if that's what God chooses but I really hope we have many many years together.

Time

May 19th, 2021

3 years and 5 months since Steve died.

8 months since Chris and I went out for the first time.

1 month until Michael and Skylar's wedding.

Time is such a weird thing. What does it mean and how do we experience it?

Last night Chris and I went to Dairy Queen for ice cream after dinner and running a couple errands. There was an elderly couple getting ice cream. The line was too long and the inside was closed so they came back in line behind us. I paid their bill for them. I asked if Chris would take me to get ice cream when I'm a pretty little old lady and he said yes but then said I'd probably have to take him because he'll have Alzheimer's and won't remember where we were going. I told him I'll take care of him. I found out his dad and Grandpa had Alzheimer's in their '70s. Chris said it's genetic. It doesn't change my love for him and confirms that I need to be in his life so that he's not alone. I think Go has everything worked out and the timing is perfect even when we don't understand it or want to accept it.

Ice Cream Plans

June 8th, 2021

I talked with Chris last night and he said he loved me so much and was kind of choked up. He said he worries that I'm going to leave him, because everyone in his life has. I told him I'm not going anywhere. I reminded him that he promised to take me for ice cream when I'm an old lady so he can't go anywhere either. I'm glad we got to talk. He felt much better this morning. I told him that I just want to make him happy.

More Time Realization

June 19th, 2021

3 and 1/2 years since Steve died.

9 months since Chris and I met.

I've been connecting with him more this week. I know he's watching over us. He still leaves me quarters in odd places and I sense his presence on my porch. I hear songs that were part of our relationship.

I'm so grateful to have a new love. Since I have been busy helping the kids, I've been missing him this week and I hope he's missed me too. I'm very appreciative of the patience he has for me to be on a grief journey and a love journey with him.

Wedding day for Michael and Skylar. I am so happy for them and yet feeling grief about Steve not being here to experience the day physically with us. I am reminded so much of our wedding day. I'm honored that Skylar made a board that has pictures of her aunt and of Steve and says "If heaven wasn't so far away, we know you would be here today". I am so happy that they are in love and making a future together.

9 Months

June 28th, 2021

We have now celebrated 9 months together and I'm so in love with Chris. He allows me to grieve. He's always there when I need someone to talk to or to get a hug. I don't feel that me being a widow or a single mom is an issue. He lets me be who I need to be when I need to be that person. He knows that being a mom comes before him a lot of the time and is very understanding. He accepts that I have a past because he does too. Everything that happened before we got together made us who we are and has allowed us to form this relationship.

I thank God everyday for the time I had with Steve and for the time I now have with Chris. I am so blessed to have two men love me completely and accept who I am.

I told Chris yesterday that I wasn't sure what I would do today or how I would be feeling because it would have been my anniversary. He told me to do whatever I wanted to do. That is the best advice anyone can give another person no matter what the situation is, if they are grieving or not.

Everyone needs to do what is right for them at the moment. Each person needs to find what works for them to heal. It's okay to not be okay and it's definitely okay to be okay. It is okay to be happy and loving life while still missing the people that have gone to heaven.

Our Space

July 8th, 2021

We talked a little bit about marriage and he said that maybe down the road because he likes what we have now. I don't think he would be with someone to even think about getting married. He did say that if I was to live at his house that he'd get another shack to clean out the other bedroom so I'd have room for my stuff. He is proud of the fact that he was able to get the land near his brother and pay it off. I think we have work to do if we are going to make it truly our space.

Only 10 Months

July 21st, 2021

I've been really thinking about our relationship and where it's going. It's only been 10 months and I absolutely love what we have so there's no rush. I know we're committed to each other for life. I know he's not interested in anyone else and I'm not either. I need to focus on us day by day and trust that the future will happen according to God's plans. I don't need to spend so much time worrying or planning for what could or should happen.

Life is for the Living

July 29th, 2021

My Aunt Karen and I were talking today about how seven years we never would have thought we would be having a conversation about dating. It's weird that we both lost our husbands. I told her that she has helped me so much by being independent and making it on her own. She told me that my dating has helped her realize that life is for the living. We agree that if the situations were reversed, we would want our husbands to live life to the fullest, to date and be happy. I sure miss both Uncle Kenny and Steve. I know my uncle visits her as an eagle. Steve visits me too with quarters.

Quarter

August 2nd, 2021

Even after my conversation with my Aunt Karen, I've been struggling lately with grief again. I know Chris and I are doing really well. While making dinner, I moved a bag of apples and underneath I found a quarter on his kitchen counter yesterday. I think it is a sign from Steve that he is okay with our relationship. I know I would want him to be with someone new and to be happy if I was the one that had passed away. I wonder what signs I would send. I hope Chris's parents are happy for us too.

Are You Getting Married?

September 23rd, 2021

A friend asked me about my relationship and when I said that things are going really well with Chris, he responded with "I am glad things are going well Chris. Are you guys going to get marrrrrrried?" I told him that I would like to and that I brought it up with Chris the other day and he said that he hadn't really thought about and liked where we are. I don't think it will happen until Matthew is done with school, so another 4 years.

I think a lot about where we will love. He's been in his house for 10 years. I don't picture us living in my house for sure as Steve and I had made so many design elements related to us being old. Plus I think Brian and Matthew might want to continue living here. I think something would really have to change for me to be able to live in his house. He has all of the space filled. Ideally I would like to purchase something together, but I'm not sure about the money part. I don't know if he would go for it.

Truly Happy

September 24th, 2021

I messaged a friend today: "I am truly happy with Chris." It makes me think about how much I grieved and worried after Steve died, but I think I knew in my heart that I could love again. So blessed that Chris said yes to picking rocks a little over a year ago.

Love Spending Time

October 21st, 2021

In talking about our life together I messaged him the following:
 " I love spending time with you and how comfortable you make me feel. I'm not going anywhere. I don't want you to be upset by anything we do. I know how hard feelings with the past can be. I really struggle to feel lovable, but you make me feel that way."
 His response:
 " I want to make good memories with you and forget my old ones. I'm happy to have you in my life."

A Different Path

December 8th, 2021

Here is what I wrote after listening to today's reflection about a poem/autobiography by Portia Nelson:

Choosing to move forward with life was very hard, it is hard. But it's made so much of a difference in me. Sometimes what seems so hard is just a lesson to choose another sidewalk if one is full of holes or has been closed. God closed the street of my marriage when Steve passed away. He forced me to choose another path. I'm still on my journey. I can turn around and see the other path. I can see all the paths I chose or were chosen for me but I can also look ahead and see the next path that's available to me. It's scary to leave the familiar path with the people in the places I'm familiar with but it's an option to always go back in my memories and relive the moments. Looking at a different direction opens up possibilities I never knew existed. Move forward and when you get to a crossroads, spend time in the moments of the path you've been on and then choose a new one to continue your journey.

No One is Perfect

April 10th, 2022

Today I talked with Chris about how I feel about my weight. He told me that it is not an issue for him. He's not only with me for my looks, He says that no one is perfect and that is why we are perfect for each other. Later on we talked about proposals and he said someday, but we have time.

Saying Yes

April 20th, 2022

30 years ago I said yes to Steve to see a movie and now I'm ready to say yes to Chris. I thought about proposing but I think I want to wait for Chris to do it. I know we've talked about no dates. I gave him a note. I still don't even know my ring size. Maybe Chris and I couldn't go to the local gift shop that makes jewelry and do something custom with my own agate or one that Chris would think would be cool.

Songs

May 5th, 2022

Heard the song "Ghost" and then "Say You Won't Let Go" with a part about being a ghost. Made me think and cry. I love Steve as a ghost. I love them both as ghosts. I love them both now. I love them both forever. I can love Chris and Steve at the same time. I will grieve and move forward. I can stop being Steve's wife. I can be with Chris.

I'm ready to let go, not forget, not be done with grief, not stop loving Steve but let go - let go of him coming back he's not, he's gone from this earth. Ready to move forward and live my life. The life I want, the life I can live. I would want to be happy and not stuck in grief. I'd want to know he was living, living out the life God gave him - the path he was chosen to walk on for as long as God decides. I'm working on trusting and accepting my intuition, the guidance for my spirit guides in the path God has put me on. I'm choosing to experience joy, love, and hope in my physical body and to do what feels right for me and for my boys and for Chris. I want Chris in my life.

Last night at the beach, I was remembering how nervous I was thinking that he'd kiss me when we went to see the sunset on our first date. I remember not knowing if it was right if I'd know how to kiss someone else and if crying would make him end it. And he just told me to take my time. He told me a lot of things, but we're both 47, not super old or young, but old enough that the tomorrows are getting less. I guess they always are. But with family history, etc I worry that we're not going to have the time to be old and gray. I do plan to love him till my lungs give out and even when we're ghosts. I'm also going to always love Steve. It doesn't end. My heart will just grow a new space.

There's Always Tomorrow

May 6th, 2022

I have heard the new song, "Ghost" by Justin Bieber, at least once a day for the past week or so. I know I'm hearing it so that I can still process my grief.

It starts off by saying, "Youngblood thinks there's always tomorrow." and then something about needing more time but time can't be borrowed. I don't just think it's the youngbloods that feel that we always get tomorrow. A lot of times I forget that we don't always get tomorrow too. And I do sometimes wish that I could have more time. I think about what I would do or say if I could even have a few more moments. I'm not sure Steve and I ever talked about more than the financial part if one of us was to pass away. We had a lot of those plans and finances in place. I don't think we talked about decisions with the kids or being in another relationship. We had put custody arrangements in our will if we both passed away.

The next part of the song is about not having you here and settling for the ghost relates to what I've been feeling a lot lately. I know that Steve is watching over me and that that's never going to end regardless of what decisions I make. But it truly is settling.

You don't get a choice. I'm just glad that he continues to visit me and let me know that his love hasn't ended.

When Steve first died, I did think about following him, but not until it was my time. I knew I was still supposed to be living; that many people still needed me; and that my life did have a purpose that I had not fulfilled yet. I miss him and I miss him being at important events but I don't miss him more than the life I have. I know I'm meant to be living without him because it has made me stronger, more independent, and able to make more decisions that are right for me and for the boys.

I wrote the first part of this and then left for work. I started my playlist and the second or third song that came on was "Say You Won't Let Go" by James Arthur. This is the song I consider our song with Chris. It hit me hard that the part I always share with Chris in that song is asking him to "say you won't let go, I wanna live with you, even when we're ghosts".

Realizing this I just said, "okay universe" I get it. I can love both people and want to be with them forever.

Thank you, God, for bringing two amazing men into my life who love me and support me!

Happy with Chris

May 8th, 2022

My friend told me today that it's good seeing me happy with Chris. I told him that I am really happy. It is great to have someone to celebrate special events with and just do the everyday ordinary things too.

Another Tattoo

May 19th, 2022

I never ever thought I would have a tattoo and then I got one in honor of Steve after he died. Tonight I got a second one. It is the same freckle pattern that Chris has on his shoulder. The artist traced his dots and then had us stand so that mine were in the same place on my arm. I told Chris when we got to the car that I had to keep him now. He said he was okay with that.

Kids or Relationship

June 26th, 2022

I told a friend today that custody will always be something that has to be discussed. I am in a constant battle inside my head. Should I spend time with my kids or spend time with Chris or should we do something all together? Sometimes Chris will come over and we'll get dinner and watch a movie or something. It will always be part of my parenting. Sometimes it's just hard when I want to spend time alone with Chris.

25th Anniversary

June 27th, 2022

I am struggling this morning, already thinking about tomorrow. June 28th is our wedding anniversary and tomorrow would be 25 years. Steve and I talked about making it that far and possibly going to Hawaii for a honeymoon because we really didn't have one when we got married.

I spent a lot of time thinking about Steve this morning and then when I went to donate blood, "The Wreck of the Edmund Fitzgerald" song came on followed by one by Bob Seger. I know Steve was just saying hello because there's no reason to play "The wreck of the Edmund Fitzgerald" other than in November on the anniversary of it sinking and Bob Seger was one of his favorite artists.

My Aunt Karen messaged me yesterday telling me that she was having a difficult time with this week too. We find it interesting that we are the only members of our family to be widows and our anniversary for our weddings is the same date. She said goodbye to my uncle on their 40th wedding anniversary 7 years ago. They got married the year that Steve and I were born.

We both feel very blessed to have a connection with each other even though the journey can be hard.

Widow Again

July 11th, 2022

I was talking with Matthew today about a comment Skylar made a few days ago. She told me how proud of me she was for moving forward and dating again and how she wasn't sure if she was to become a widow if she could do it. His response to this was something like, you got through it once so you know you can do it again.

I feel deep down that I will again be a widow. I treasure the time I do have with Chris because I know that any moment it can end. But the love that we share makes whatever time we have together absolutely worth it. I recommend falling in love again if your spouse dies.

Is it sometimes hard to hope that we'll make it 25 years when I didn't get that with Steve? Yes! But without hope and love, what do we have?

Sick Again

September 11th, 2022

I'm trying to give myself grace but I'm super frustrated. Yesterday Chris and I tried to walk and pick rocks and I did not make it very far before I had to go back to the car. Walking is still such an effort. He is super patient with me but I'm not super patient with myself.

2 Years

September 19th, 2022

Two years since we met.

Two years that I have been in love again.

Two years of continuing to learn who I am as a person and a partner.

Two years learning about how to grow our relationship.

Two years ago I was so worried about meeting someone, even though he was local and we knew family members. I just think how worrying was all for nothing. He and I connected right away.

I do believe it might have been love at first sight...or maybe love after three hours. I still get excited when I see him. I love being with him even if it is just to watch TV or drive to see the sunset.

Bring Up Memories

October 10th, 2022

I was talking with a coworker today and Steve's name came up on some paperwork. She said she was hesitant to bring it up with me because she didn't want to make me sad. I told her that I am happy when people tell me a story about him. It means he is not forgotten. It means he was important to people.

I so appreciate that Chris allows me to tell stories about Steve or about our marriage. That part of my life is not gone because Steve died. It is my past. I love hearing about when Chris was younger and although his life does not usually involve a romantic relationship it still gives me insight into who he is and why.

Loss as a Trigger

November 5th, 2022

I heard that a friend's step dad passed away. I told her boyfriend that this might be a huge trigger for her. She had lost her husband over a year ago. Another loss can be a tigger and bring back lots of the grief from the past. She may really be reminded of the events surrounding his death and struggle with attending the funeral and even processing this grief as it is all different.

Engaged?

December 4th, 2022

Chris and I had a long conversion today about getting engaged. He said soon and then I said I wasn't sure about the marriage part yet. I think one of the reasons is because Matthew is still only 16. He then said we could get married when we are old. I laughed as I thought about us being in our 80s. I said we don't have to ever get married, but he felt that we need to because I want to. I told him marriage is when both people want it and if he is not ready, then we won't. He said he never really thought he would be with someone that he wanted to marry. I told him that we can be engaged or maybe do a commitment ring. He thought that sounded like a better idea.

   I had a dream of the two of us by the water at sunset and someone was taking our picture. I wonder if this is the commitment ceremony where we agree to be together forever. (Although maybe he doesn't want a ring.)

Your Husband

December 11th, 2022

Today we went to breakfast and when we were done, he went to pay the bill and I used the restroom. When I came out I was waiting by the door as I assumed he was in the restroom. A woman caught my eye and said, "Your husband went out to the car already." I smiled and thanked her. When I got in the car, I told Chris that we got married over breakfast and told him what the woman had said. He smiled and said "okay".

Doing Great

December 13th, 2022

Chris and I are still doing great. We are looking at the future and maybe something more like a commitment not engagement.

I'm having moments of grief here and there as we approach the five year mark. Some days it's really hard to believe that it's been that long and other days it feels like yesterday.

Budgeting

December 15th, 2022

I went to the bank today with Brian and were talking about finances and really thinking about how I'm only where I am because of how much Steve did with planning in our budgeting and because of his death. I've been thinking a lot about him as we approach the 5-year mark on Monday.

Commitment Ceremony

February 11th, 2023

We went for a beautiful drive today and took lots of photos of the lake and the ice, had a Valentine's Day dinner and then stopped and took more pictures of the amazing sunset.

In the car I asked him if I could tell him what I had been thinking about. I told him that I would love to do a commitment ceremony with him in September on the beach, just the two of us with maybe my cousin who is a photographer there to record it. He said that sounded good and that he would order me an agate ring. I told him that we could find the perfect agate together this summer. There is a company I follow on facebook that makes custom jewelry out of people's stones, usually agates.

I looked at the calendar and our three year anniversary will be on a Tuesday. I really think we're going to have to wait until much closer to pick the date and we can see what the weather is going to be like. I would love it to be a beautiful evening with a gorgeous sunset and that's not always predictable.

I wonder what people say during a commitment ceremony and do they write something of their own or do they find something pre-made? I also wonder about music and what we would wear and those things but I think we wait until closer to talk about that.

I never thought when I got married to Steve that I would be thinking of making a commitment to another person. I am so blessed and grateful that I have found Chris and that he wants to be committed to me forever.

I watched a movie today. When the couple got married, one of the vows they said was that they would love each other as long as they both lived. Even when one of you dies you still love that person. So it truly is as long as you both live.

I pray that I do not have to be a widow again until I'm at least in my '80s. I know I can survive it, but I really don't want to.

*The cover photo is from this night. Esry Park, Copper Harbor, Michigan

Epilogue

February 21st, 2023

Steve delivered a message to me. He said he wants a white folding chair at the commitment ceremony.

Acknowledgments

Thank you Steve. Thank you for making sure we were all set. Thank you for teaching me to budget to spend what we've got and to save for future expenses and the unexpected. Thank you for always loving and being supportive of me. Thanks for being my amazing partner. I miss you. I love you. Thanks for being okay with me moving forward. I know you've always wanted me to be happy and Chris makes me happy. He's so loving and allows me to grieve and share about my life with you. I know you believe so strongly in marriage and I thought I did too but I want to be with Chris until death do us part but because he's unsure about marriage, it's not on the table right now and I'm okay with that. Thank you for teaching me to love and accept myself. Thank you for protecting me and always being there for a hug. Thank you for always being around now and watching over all of us. I feel your presence and love. Please don't ever stop loving me.

Thank you Chris. I love you so much and I'm so happy you said yes to learning to pick agates. Thank you for letting me take my time to move forward in our relationship and for being so supportive. Thank you for letting me talk about Steve and our marriage. Thanks for letting me be a mom when that's who I need to be. Thank you for wanting a future with me. Thank you for finding me attractive and for accepting me for who I am. You've always said we each have a past and I'm so happy that my past has allowed me to be with you. I love you and want to be your partner for the rest of your life or mine. I accept that I might become a widow again. I accepted our lives will be what is meant to be. I believe God has a plan and it was for me to be Steve's wife first and then to be with you. I love you and I always will.

Thank you Auntie Karen for showing me it is okay to be independent. And also to be okay and have happy moments even after your spouse died. I know Uncle Kenny and Steve shake their heads at us often and are for sure watching over us.

Thank you Mike for being brave to move forward even when people questioned it. There are no rules or timelines with grief and relationships.. Seeing your relationship has allowed me to follow my heart in many situations and not worry so much about what others think.

Thank you to all of my immediate and extended family (from birth, through adoption and through marriage) for accepting me, my grief and supporting my choice to move forward. I love you all.

About Author

Emilie is a mom to three young men and a daughter-in-law, an educator, an author, a nature photographer, and a writer. Emilie taught special education for 20 years before taking a new job at the ISD. She now is the compliance monitor, technical assistance provider and transition coordinator. Relationships and faith are most important to her. She is an outgoing person who loves quiet time on the beach with God, her camera, and a journal. One of her favorite hobbies is finding agates and omars on the beach.

After her husband passed away in December of 2018, she started a blog, grieffaithandfinances.com. Writing and journaling has one of the ways she processes her emotions and questions. She has since published three books about her journey through grief, the miracles she's experienced and about finding love again.

Emilie, in addition to writing, takes nature photography, mostly of the beautiful Upper Peninsula of Michigan and Lake Superior. Many of her unedited photos can be viewed on Instagram @upuneditedphotography. Her dream job is being a photographer for the national parks.

Also By Emilie Lancour

"It's Okay to be Okay; Finding Joy through Grief"

"It's Okay to Love Again"

"A Cup of Miracles"

Resources

Ted Talk by Nora McInerny "We don't move on from grief, we move forward with it." :

https://www.ted.com/talks/nora_mcinerny_we_don_t_move_on_from_grief_we_move_forward_with_it?utm_campaign=tedspread&utm_medium=referral&utm_source=tedcomshare

Lyrics to songs mentioned:

"Ghost" by Justin Beiber: https://www.azlyrics.com/lyrics/justinbieber/ghost.html

"Say You Won't Let Go" by James Arthur: https://www.azlyrics.com/lyrics/jamesarthur/sayyouwontletgo.html

Made in the USA
Monee, IL
08 April 2023